Anonymous

Proceedings of a Convocation of Knights Templar

and of the Grand Commandery of Knights Templar and the appendant

orders of the State of Alabama

Anonymous

Proceedings of a Convocation of Knights Templar
and of the Grand Commandery of Knights Templar and the appendant orders of the State of Alabama

ISBN/EAN: 9783337298258

Printed in Europe, USA, Canada, Australia, Japan

Cover: Foto ©ninafisch / pixelio.de

More available books at **www.hansebooks.com**

PROCEEDINGS

OF A

CONVOCATION OF KNIGHTS TEMPLAR

AND OF

The Grand Commandery

OF

KNIGHTS TEMPLAR,

AND

THE APPENDANT ORDERS

OF THE

STATE OF ALABAMA.

First Conclave held at the City of Montgomery, December
1st, A. D. 1860, A. O. 742.

MONTGOMERY, ALA.
DAILY POST BOOK AND JOB OFFICE.
1861.

CONVOCATION

OF

KNIGHTS TEMPLAR.

PURSUANT to previous notice, the representatives of four Commanderies of Knights Templar and the Appendant Orders, existing in the State of Alabama under Charters from the Grand Encampment of the United States of America, assembled in the Asylum of *Montgomery Commandery, No. 4*, at the City of Montgomery, on Thursday, the 29th day of November, A. D., 1860, A. O., 742, at 7 o'clock, P. M., for the purpose of organizing a Grand Commandery of Knights Templar and the Appendant Orders for the State of Alabama.

The following Sir Knights were present :

SIR RICHARD F. KNOTT, of Mobile Commandery, No. 2, Mobile.
" PELEG BROWN,   "   "   "   "   "
" LEWIS B. THORNTON, of Tuscumbia, " No. 3, Tuscumbia.
" HUGH P. WATSON, of Montgomery, " No. 4, Montgomery.
" EDMUND M. HASTINGS,   "   "   "   "
" RICHARD FRASER,   "   "   "   "   "
" THOMAS WELSH,   "   "   "   "   "
" ABRAM J. WALKER,   "   "   "   .   "   "
" JOHN H. WILLOUGHBY.   "   "   "   "
" B. MASSIE,   "   "   "   "   "
" NOAH B. CLOUD,   "   "   "   "   "
" HENRY P. LEE,   "   "   "   "   "
" BENJ. S. THIESS,   "   "   "   "   "
" JAMES B. HARRISON,   Selma.   "   No. 5, Selma.

Sir Hugh P. Watson, Commander of Montgomery, Commandery, No. 4, stated the object of the Convocation, and on his motion, Sir Richard F. Knott, Generalissimo of Mobile Commandery, No. 2, was invited to preside during its deliberations, and Sir James B. Harrison, was appointed Recorder of the Convocation.

On motion of Sir E. M. Hastings,

Resolved, That a Committee of three be appointed to examine the credentials of those claiming seats in this Convocation.

The presiding officer named the following Knights as such Committee:

On Credentials,.......... { Sir E. M. HASTINGS,
Sir PELEG BROWN,
Sir JAMES B. HARRISON.

The Committee after a brief recess presented the following report:

To the Convocation now in session :

The Committee on Credentials having attended to the duty assigned them, respectfully report :

That there are Five Commanderies in the State, working under Charters granted by the Grand Encampment of the United States, and that they are represented in the Convocation as follows :

Mobile, No. 2, by...... { Sir R. F. KNOTT, proxy for the E. Com'r.
Sir R. F. KNOTT, Generalissimo,
Sir PELEG BROWN, proxy for the C. G.

Tuscumbia, No. 3, by Sir LEWIS B. THORNTON, proxy for E. C.

Montg'ery, No. 4, by { Sir HUGH P. WATSON, E. Com'r.
Sir E. M. HASTINGS, proxy for the Gen.
Sir A. J. WALKER, Captain General.

Selma, No. 5, by... { Sir JAMES B. HARRISON, E. Com'r.
Sir WM. S. KNOX, Generalissimo.
Sir A. J. GOODWIN, Captain General.

All of which is respectfully submitted.

E. M. HASTINGS,
PELEG BROWN,   } Committee.
J. B. HARRISON,

Which report was received and concurred in, and the Committee discharged.

On motion of Sir E. M. Hastings,

Resolved, That all Sir Knights in good standing are cordially invited to be present during the deliberations of the Convocation.

Sir Richard F. Knott, presiding officer of the Convocation presented the warrant received from the Most Eminent Grand Master of the Order in the United States, authorizing the formation of a State Grand Commandery, which was read by the Recorder, and is as follows:

BENJAMIN BROWN FRENCH,

Grand Master of Knights Templar of the United States of America.

Know Ye, That, Whereas, there are established in the State of Alabama Five Commanderies of Knights Templar, regularly chartered by the Grand Encampment of the United States, and now working under its jurisdiction, to-wit: *Washington, No.* 1, at Marion ; *Mobile,* No. 2, at Mobile , *Tuscumbia, No.* 3, at Tuscumbia ; *Montgomery, No.* 4, at Montgomery, and *Selma, No.* 5, at Selma: and whereas the said Commanderies, or at least three of them, are desirous to form a Grand Commandery of Knights Templar, for the State of Alabama ; and the Grand Encampment of the United States having, at its last Triennial session, granted its authority to the Commanderies aforesaid to establish a Grand Commandery in said State, and due application having been made to me therefor, *Now Know Ye, That I Benjamin B. French,* Grand Master as aforesaid, by virtue of the high powers in me vested, and in order to carry out the authority granted by the Grand Encampment, do authorize and empower the Commanderies aforesaid, or any three of them, at their pleasure within said State, and then and there to establish, form and organize a Grand Commandery of Knights Templar, subordinate to our said Grand Encampment, to be known and designated as *"The Grand Commandery of Knights Templar of the State of Alabama,"* to be conducted in accordance with such Constitution, rules and regulations as said Grand Commandery may see fit to form and adopt: *Provided,* the same shall not be repugnant to the Constitution of the Grand Encampment of the United States, or the general principles and usages of the order.

The said Grand Commandery will make due return of the proceedings at the formation thereof, and of the Grand Officers, to me and to our V. E. Grand Recorder.

And for forming, organizing and holding said Grand Commandery, this shall be their sufficient *Warrant.*

Given under my hand, and private seal at Rainsford Island, in Boston Harbor, this fourth day of September, Anno Domini, 1860, A. O. 742.

B. B. FRENCH, [L. S.]
GRAND MASTER.

On motion of Sir H. P. Watson, the Convocation was then adjourned until to-morrow at 7 o'clock, P. M.

IN CONVOCATION.

FRIDAY, 7 o'CLOCK, P. M.,
November 30, A. D., 1860, A. O. 742.

The Convocation assembled, pursuant to adjournment, Sir Richard F. Knott presiding.

On motion of Sir E. M. Hastings,

Resolved, That a committee, composed of one from each Commandery represented, be appointed to prepare, and present, for the consideration of the Convocation, a Constitution, or Code of Statutes, for the government of the Grand Commandery about to be formed.

Whereupon the following Sir Knights were appointed said committee: Sir E. M. Hastings, of Montgomery, No. 4, Sir

Peleg Brown, Mobile, No. 2, Sir Lewis B. Thornton, Tuscumbia, No. 3, and Sir James B. Harrison, Selma, No. 5.

The committee, after a brief recess, made the following Report:

To the Convocation now in session :—

The committee appointed to prepare and report a Constitution, or Code of Statutes, for the government of the Grand Commandery about to be formed, have performed the duty assigned them, and submit herewith a Code of Statutes, and recommend their adoption as the Statutes of the Grand Commandery of Knights Templar, and the Appendant Orders of the State of Alabama.

All of which is respectfully submitted.

E. M. HASTINGS,
P. BROWN,
L. B. THORNTON,
J. B. HARRISON,
} Committee.

The report was received, and the *Statutes, having been taken up and considered seperately, the whole were unanimously adopted, and the committee discharged.

On motion of Sir H. P. Watson,

Resolved, That this Convocation do now proceed to the election of officers of the Grand Commandery.

Sir E. M. Hastings and Sir Peleg Brown were appointed tellers, and the following officers were elected:

Sir RICHARD F. KNOTT, of Mobile, Grand Commander,

" STERLING A. M. WOOD, of Florence, Dep. Grand Com'r.

" JAMES B. HARRISON, of Selma, Grand Generalissimo.

" PELEG BROWN, of Mobile, Grand Captain General,

" HENRY TALBIRD, of Marion, Grand Prelate,

" PORTER KING, of Marion, Grand Senior Warden,

" LEWIS B. THORNTON, of Tuscumbia, Grand Jr. Warden,

" HUGH P. WATSON, of Montgomery, Grand Treasurer,

" EDMUND M. HASTINGS, of Montgomery, Grand Recorder,

" JOHN H. PIPPIN, of Mobile, Grand Standard Bearer,

" WILLIAM S. KNOX, of Selma, Grand Sword Bearer,

---

* For Statutes see page 14.—K. M. H., Rec.

" JOSEPH M. WILLIAMS, of Montgomery, Grand Warder,

" JOSEPH McGAW, of Mobile, Grand Sentinel.

The Recorder read a communication from the Grand Master of the order authorizing ———— as his proxy, to instal the officers elect of the Grand Commandery ; and upon motion of Sir H. P. Watson the blank therein was filled with the name of Sir William Field, R;. E:. Grand Commander of the Grand Commandery of Massachusetts and Rhode Island.

On motion of Sir H. P. Watson,

Resolved, That the Grand Commandery of the State of Alabama be opened at three o'clock, P. M., on Saturday, the first day of December, A. D., 1860, A. O., 742, and that the present Convocation be adjourned *sine die*.

J. B. HARRISON,

Recorder.

GRAND COMMANDERY

OF

Knights Templar and the Appendant Orders,

OF THE

STATE OF ALABAMA.

FIRST CONCLAVE.

The Grand Commandery of Knights Templar and the Appendant Orders of the State of Alabama commenced its First Conclave at the Asylum of Montgomery Commandery No. 4, in the City of Montgomery, on Saturday, the first day of December, *Anno Domini* 1860, *Anno Ordinis* 742, at three o'clock, P. M.

Present:

R∴ E∴ Sir RICHARD F. KNOTT,....*Grand Commander,*

V∴ E∴ Sir WILLIAM FIELD,...........as *Deputy Grand Com'r.*

E∴ Sir JAMES B. HARRISON,.........*Grand Generalissimo,*

E∴ Sir PELEG BROWN,................*Grand Captain Gen'l,*

E∴ Sir JOHN H. WILLOUGHBY,. .as *Grand Prelate,*

E∴ Sir NOAH B. CLOUD,............as *Grand Senior Warden,*

E∴ Sir LEWIS B. THORNTON,.........*Grand Junior Warden,*

E∴ Sir HUGH P. WATSON,...........*Grand Treasurer,*

E∴ Sir EDMUND M. HASTINGS,.......*Grand Recorder,*

E∴ Sir GEORGE D. NORRIS,..........as *Grand Stand. Bearer,*

E∴ Sir JAMES M. BRUNDIDGE, ...as *Grand Sword Bearer,*

E∴ Sir JOSEPH M. WILLIAMS,.........*Grand Warder,*

Sir THOMAS McDOUGAL,......as *Grand Sentinel;*

2

And a number of visiting Knights, who were invited to be present.

Mobile Commandery, No. 2, Tuscumbia, No. 3, Montgomery, No. 4, and Selma, No. 5, being represented, the Grand Commandery was opened in *Ample and Knightly form*, with prayer by the Grand Prelate.

The minutes of the proceedings of the Convocation held on the twenty-ninth and thirtieth ultimo, were read, and the statutes adopted in Convocation, and the officers elected in accordance therewith, were approved and adopted by the Grand Commandery.

On motion of Sir H. P. Watson, the Grand Commander of the Grand Commandery of Massachusetts and Rhode Island, then took the chair, and under the authority of a warrant from Hon. Sir Benjamin Brown French, Grand Master of Knights Templar in the United States, then installed Sir Richard F. Knott, R:. E:. Grand Commander of the Grand Commandery of the State of Alabama, and proceeded to install all the rest of the Grand Officers present.

The Right Eminent Grand Commander resumed the chair and gave notice that, either in person or by proxy, he would install those absent, viz: Sir Sterling A. M. Wood, Sir Henry Talbird, Sir Porter King, Sir John H. Pippin, Sir William S. Knox, and Sir Joseph McGaw, in their respective Commanderies.

On motion of Sir James B. Harrison,

Resolved, That the several Commanderies in this State, heretofore working under the jurisdiction of the Grand Encapment of the United States of America, be, and are hereby authorised to continue work under their original charters ; and that they shall rank and be registered as follows : viz:

Washington Com'ndery, No. 1, at Marion, Perry County,
Mobile   "   " 2, " Mobile, Mobile   "
Tuscumbia   "   " 3, " Tuscumbia, Fra'lin   "
Montgomery   "   " 4, " Montg'y., Montg'y   "
Selma   "   " 5, " Selma, Dallas   "

and, that the Charters of said Commanderies be endorsed, or

countersigned, within the ensuing twelve months, by the R:
E:. Grand Commander, attested by the Grand Recorder, with
the seal of the Grand Commandery.

On motion of Sir E. M. Hastings,

Resolved, That the Grand Commander, Deputy Grand Commander and Grand Captain General be, and are hereby appointed a Committee, with power to devise and have prepared,
as early as possible, a seal for this Grand Commandery.

On motion of Sir H. P. Watson,

Resolved, That five hundred copies of the proceedings of the
late Convocation and at this conclave be printed under the su-
perintendence of the Grand Recorder ; that twenty-five copies
thereof be transmitted to each subordinate Commandery, two
copies to each Grand Commandery in North America, one
copy each to the first four officers and Grand Recorder of the
Grand Encampment of the United States, and to such other
eminent Sir Knights as may be deemed advisable, reserving
at least one hundred copies for future disposal by the Grand
Commandery.

On motion of Sir L. B. Thornton,

Resolved, That each of the five Commanderies now under
the jurisdiction of this Grand Commandery be directed to forward to the Grand Recorder thereof, as soon as possible after the
close of this conclave, copies of its charter, together with a
return of its officers and members at the date of the organization of the Grand Commandery, that the same may be pub-
lished with the proceedings ; and that a complete return to
that date, shall at the said time be made by each to the Grand
Recorder of the Grand Encampment of the United States, and
be accompanied by such dues as may have accrued to that
body.

On motion of Sir Jos. M. Williams,

Resolved, That, to defray the expense of printing the pro-
cbedings of the Grand Commandery, and other necessary expenses attending its organization, the Grand Recorder shall certify the amounts, when ascertained, to the R:. E:. Grand
Commander, who shall apportion the same among the several

subordinate Commanderies in proportion to the membership of each, which sums shall be transmitted and paid over to the Grand Recorder immediately after receiving notification of the amount.

On motion of Sir James B. Harrison.

Resolved, That the Grand Recorder be directed to prepare and have printed with the proceedings, a form of petition for the establishment of a subordinate Commandery, and of application for the orders of Knighthood, and for affiliation; and such further forms for returns and other purposes as may be required.

On motion of Sir L. B. Thornton.

Resolved, That a Committee on Foreign Correspondence, consisting of one from each Commandery, be appointed by the R:. E:. Grand Commander, to report at our next Grand Annual Conclave.

The Grand Commander named the following Sir Knights as such Committee:

Commmittee on Foreign Correspondence:	Sir A. J. WALKER, Com'ry No. 4,
	" L. B. THORNTON, " " 3,
	" PORTER KING, " " 1,
	" PELEG BROWN, " " 2,
	" BENJ. J. HARRISON, " " 5,

On motion of Sir H. P. Watson,

Resolved, That the thanks of this Grand Commandey are eminently due, and they are hereby tendered, to our venerable brother, the R:. E:. Sir William Field, for the efficient aid rendered by him in the organization and installation of its officers.

There being no further business, the minutes of this session were read and approved, and with prayer by the Grand Prelate, the Grand Commandery was closed in ample and Knightly form.

A true copy of the proceedings of the Convocation and Conclave, as before mentioned.

WITNESS my signature, with the Seal of our Grand Commandery, and the attestation of our Grand Recorder.

RICHARD F. KNOTT,
Grand Commander.

Attest,
E. M. HASTINGS,
Grand Recorder.

STATUTES

OF THE

Grand Commandery of Knights Templar,

AND THE

APPENDANT ORDERS

OF THE

STATE OF ALABAMA.

———•———

CHAPTER I.

RELATIVE TO THE GRAND COMMANDERY.

I.

Of its Title and Seal.

This body shall be entitled "The Grand Commandery of Knights Templar, and the Appendant Orders of the State of Alabama," and shall have a seal, bearing suitable devices and inscriptions, which shall be affixed to all instruments issued by or under its authority.

II.

Of its Officers and Members.

The Grand Commandery shall be composed of a Grand Commander (whose address is *Right Eminent*); a Deputy Grand Commander (whose address is *Very Eminent*); a Grand Generalissimo; a Grand Captain General; a Grand Prelate; a Grand Senior Warden; a Grand Junior Warden; a Grand

Treasurer; a Grand Recorder; a Grand Standard Bearer; a Grand Sword Bearer; a Grand Warder (whose several addresses are *Eminent*); a Grand Captain of the Guards, (the Sentinel); all Past Grand Commanders, Past Deputy Grand Commanders, Past Grand Generalissimos, and Past Grand Captains General of this Grand Commandery; all Past Commanders, by service, of chartered Commanderies under its jurisdiction; and the Commanders, Generalissimos and Captains General, for the time, of the several chartered and duly constituted Commanderies subordinate thereto.

III.

Of Qualifications for Office or Membership.

Every officer and member of the Grand Commandery must be a member of some Commandery under its jurisdiction; and with the suspension or cessation of such membership, shall cease his office and membership in the Grand Commandery.

IV.

Of its Powers and Authority.

The Grand Commandery derives all its powers from the Grand Encampment of Knights Templar and the Appendant Orders of the United States of America, to the Constitution and Regulations of which, its obedience is ever due. Under these powers it has authority over all Commanderies, Knights Templar, and Knights of the Appendant Orders within the State of Alabama. It may grant Dispensations and Charters for forming and holding Commanderies therein, and at its pleasure, may arrest, suspend, or revoke them It may enact such statutes, and pass such orders, for its own government and for that of its subordinates and the Knights within its jurisdiction, as shall not conflict with the Constitution and Regulations of the Grand Encampment; may alter, amend or annul the same, and may exercise all other authority which shall be deemed necessary for the good of the Order in this State, and which shall be in conformity with its precepts and the Constitution and Regulations of the Grand Encampment.

V.

Of its Conclaves.

The Grand Commandery shall hold an Annual Conclave, for the transaction of its regular business at the City of Montgomery commencing on the Saturday before the first Monday in December at 10 o'clock, A. M. Special Conclaves may be ordered by the Grand Commander, at his discretion, but no business shall be transacted thereat, other than that specified in such order.

VI.

Of its Elections.

The officers of the Grand Commandery shall be chosen by ballot at the Conclave to be holden immediately after the adoption of these Statutes, and thereafter at each Annual Conclave; shall be duly installed before the close thereof; and shall hold their respective offices (except as hereinbefore provided) until their successors are elected and installed. A majority of all the votes cast shall be necessary for a choice. Any vacancy in office occurring when the Grand Commandery is not in Conclave, may be filled by the Grand Commander, and the officer so appointed shall possess all the powers and be charged with all the duties of one regularly elected.

VII

Of Proxies.

Any member of the Grand Commandery, except Past Commanders and the Grand Captain of the Guards, may appear and vote by proxy ; but such proxy must, at the time of service, be a member of the same Commandery as his principal, and must present a properly authenticated certificate of his appointment.

VIII.

Of Voting.

Each member of the Grand Commandery present shall be entitled to one vote, and all questions shall be determined by a majority of votes. In case the votes are equally divided, the Grand Commander, in addition to his proper vote, shall give the casting vote.

IX.

Of Revenue.

The revenue of the Grand Commandery shall be derived from fees charged for Dispensations, Charters, Diplomas, and other instruments issued under its authority, as follows:

1. For a Dispensation, *eighty-five* dollars, of which *ten* dollars shall be the fee of the Grand Recorder;

2. For a Charter, *fifteen* dollars, of which five dollars shall be the fee of the Grand Recorder;

3. For a Diploma, five dollars, of which three shall be the fee of the Grand Recorder:

And from the following contributions levied upon the several Commanderies:

1. For each Order of the Red Cross conferred, one dollar;

2. For each Order of the Temple conferred, one dollar;

3. For each Knight Templar borne upon the rolls at the date of the Annual Returns; one dollar.

X.

Of Committees.

The following regular Committees, to consist of three members each, shall be appointed by the Grand Commander at each Annual Conclave, viz: On Credentials, on Reports of the Grand Officers, on Appeals and Grievances, on Finances and Accounts, on New Commanderies, and on Returns of Subordinates. The Grand Commander may also appoint such Special Committees at any Conclave, as may be deemed expedient by the Grand Commandery.

3

CHAPTER II.

XI.

Of the Grand Commander.

The Grand Commander shall, at each Annual Conclave, present a written report of all his official acts during the year, and of the condition of the Order within his jurisdiction, together with such recommendations as he shall deem conducive to its prosperity and advancement. He shall have a watchful supervision over the Subordinate Commanderies, and shall carefully see that the Constitution and Regulations of the Grand Encampment, and the Statutes and Orders of the Grand Commandery, are duly and promptly observed. He shall have power, when the Grand Commandery is not in Conclave, to issue dispensations, for the formation of new Commanderies, as hereinafter provided ; and shall, either in person or by proxy, constitute all new Commanderies when chartered, and install their officers. He may order special Conclaves, at his discretion, specifying the object thereof. He may visit and preside in any Commandery within his jurisdiction, and give such orders and instructions as he may deem necessary, and as shall not be inconsistent with the enactments of the Grand Encampment and Grand Commandery. He may arrest the Charter, or Dispensation of any Commandery for good reasons shown, and for proper cause may suspend any Commander from the functions of his office until the next Annual Conclave. It shall be his duty, either in person or by proxy, to attend all meetings of the Grand Encampment ; and there shall be no appeal to the Grand Commandery from his decisions.

XII.

Of the Deputy Grand Commander.

The Deputy Grand Commander, in the absence of the Grand Commander from any Conclave, shall take command : and, in the event of the death, absence from the State, or inability to serve, from any cause, of the Grand Commander, he shall succeed to, and be charged with all the powers and duties of that officer. At all other times he shall perform such duties as may be assigned him by the Grand Commandery or Grand Commander ; and he is required either in person or by proxy, to attend all meetings of the Grand Encampment.

XIII.

Of the Grand Generalissimo and Grand Captain General.

The Grand Generalissimo and Grand Captain General, in the absence of their superiors from any Conclave, shall severally take command in the order of their rank, and in the event of the death, removal from the State, or inability to serve, from any cause, of their superiors, shall in like manner succeed to, and be charged with, all the powers and duties of the Grand Commander. At all other times, they shall perform such duties as may be assigned them by the Grand Commandery or Grand Commander ; and they are required, either in person or by proxy, to attend all meetings of the Grand Encampment.

XIV.

Of the Grand Treasurer.

The Grand Treasurer shall receive all moneys belonging to the Grand Commandery from the Grand Recorder, and shall pay the same out under such regulations as by it may be provided. He shall keep a just record thereof in proper books, and at each Annual Conclave shall present a detailed account of his receipts and disbursements, together with vouchers for the last, and a full statement of the existing condition of the finances. He shall execute and file with the Grand Recorder.

within fifteen days after his installation, a bond, in such terms, in such penal sum, and with such sureties, as shall be approved by the Grand Commander, conditioned that he will faithfully discharge the duties of his office.

XV.

Of the Grand Recorder.

The Grand Recorder shall keep an accurate record of all the transactions of the Grand Commandery which should be written. He shall collect the revenue, and pay it over to the Grand Treasurer. He shall present a detailed report of his receipts, and all business appertaining to his office, at each Annual Conclave. He shall, as soon as practicable, after each Annual Conclave, transmit copies of the transactions thereat to the Grand Master of the Order, the Grand Recorder of the Grand Encampment, the Grand Recorder of the several Grand Commanderies under the jurisdiction of that body, and the Recorders of the several Commanderies within this jurisdiction. He shall keep the Seal of the Grand Commandery, and shall affix it, with his attestation, to all instruments emanating from that body and to all Dispensations issued by the Grand Commander. He shall conduct the correspondence of the Grand Commandery, and shall present at each Annual Conclave a summary of such proceedings of other Grand Commanderies as may have come into his possession.

He shall report at each Annual Conclave all unfinished business, and shall perform such other duties as may be assigned him by the Grand Commandery or Grand Commander. He shall receive such compensation for his services as the Grand Commandery may direct; and shall execute and file with the Grand Treasurer, within fifteen days after his installation, a bond, in such terms, in such penal sum, and with such sureties, as shall be approved by the Grand Commander, conditioned that he will faithfully discharge the duties of his office.

XVI.

Of the other Grand Officers.

The duties of the remaining Grand Officers, shall be such as traditionally appertain to their respective stations, and shall correspond as nearly as may be, to those of the officers of similar rank in the Grand Encampment. In case all the four principal Grand Officers shall be absent from any Conclave, the Past Grand Officers of like rank, shall, in the order of their rank and seniority, be empowered to take command.

CHAPTER III.

RELATIVE TO SUBORDINATE COMMANDERIES.

XVII

Of their Formation.

Upon the petition of nine or more Knights Templar, in good standing, the Grand Commandery, or the Grand Commander, may issue a Letter of Dispensation, authorizing them to form and open a Commandery of Knights Templar and the Appendant Orders, and to hold the same until the next Annual Conclave. But no such Dispensation shall issue unless the petition be accompanied by a recommendation from the Commandery nearest the location of the proposed new one, which shall certify to the good standing of each of the petitioners, to the proper qualifications of the Officers, whom they have nominated, and that a suitable place of assembling has been provided. The Dispensation, thus issued, shall be returned at the next Annual Conclave, together with the Book of Records, By-Laws, and Returns, when, if the transactions of the new Commandery shall appear satisfactory, it may, upon petition, receive a Charter.

XVIII.

Of Whom Composed.

A Commandery consists of a Commander, (whose address is *Eminent*), a Generalissimo, a Captain General, a Prelate, a Senior Warden, a Junior Warden, a Treasurer, a Recorder, a Standard Bearer, a Sword Bearer, a Warder, a Captain of the Guards, (the Sentinel), three Guards, and as many members as may be found convenient for work or discipline.

XIX.

Of Assemblies.

Each Commandery shall hold a stated Assembly at least once in six months, for the transaction of its regular business. Special assemblies may be ordered by the Commander, at his discretion, but no business shall be done thereat other than that specified in the order. A failure to assemble for twelve successive months shall be deemed sufficient cause for the arrest or revocation of its Charter.

XX.

Of Elections.

The officers of each Commandery (except the Sentinel and Guards, who shall be appointed by the Commander), shall be chosen by ballot at the first stated assembly in the month of November, in each year, and shall be installed before, or at the next stated assembly. A majority of all the votes cast shall be necessary for a choice.

XXI.

Of Voting.

All questions in a Commandery shall be determined by a majority of votes. Each member present shall be entitled to one vote, and when the votes are equally divided (except in elections), the Commander shall, in addition, have the casting vote.

XXII.

Of Qualifications for the Orders.

No Commandery shall confer an Order of Knighthood upon any one who is not a regular Royal Arch Mason, according to the requirements of the General Grand Chapter of the United States of America, nor unless he shall have produced evidence of his good standing at the time of application ; and no application for the Orders shall be received by any Commandery, from one who within twelve months next preceding, shall have been rejected by any Commandery, nor unless the applicant shall have resided one year next preceding in the State, and three months next preceding within its jurisdiction, except by permission of the Commandery nearest his place of residence.

XXIII.

Of Fees and Dues.

No Commandery shall confer the several Orders of Knighthood for a less fee than thirty dollars, and no application therefor shall be received unless accompanied by such fee. The dues of the members of each Commandery shall be such as may be provided in its By-Laws, and the non-payment of such dues for a period of twelve months, unless good reasons therefor be shown, shall be punished by suspension.

XXIV.

Of the Commander.

Each Commander has it in special charge to see that the By-Laws of his Commandery, the Statutes and Orders of the Grand Commandery, and the Constitution and Regulations of the Grand Encampment, are duly observed by the Knights under his command ; that accurate records are kept, and just accounts and proper reports rendered by his officers; and that regular returns are annually made to the Grand Commandery at the time prescribed therefor, with prompt payment of the annual dues. From his decisions there shall be no appeal to the Commandery, but any five members thereof may complain of his decisions or conduct to the Grand Commandery, or Grand Commander. It shall be his duty either in person or by proxy, to attend all Conclaves of the Grand Commandery.

XXV.

Of the Generalissimo and Captain General.

The Generalissimo and Captain General shall perform the duties severally assigned them by the traditional usages of the Order ; and in the absence of the Commander, shall, in the order of their rank, succeed to, and be charged with, all his powers and duties. It shall be the duty of both, either in person or by proxy, to attend all Conclaves of the Grand Commandery. In the absence of all the three principal officers, the Past Commanders, in the order of their seniority may take command.

XXVI.

Of the Treasurer and Recorder.

The Treasurer shall receive from the Recorder and safely keep all moneys belonging to the Commandery ; and shall pay the same out under such regulations, and account therefor at such times and in such manner, as by it may be prescribed. The Recorder shall keep an accurate record of all the transactions of the Commandery which should be written, including a list of the officers, members and visitors present at each assembly , shall collect the revenue and pay it over to the Treasurer , shall keep correct accounts of the dues of members ; shall prepare and transmit the annual returns to the Grand Recorder ; shall keep the seal of the Commandery, and affix it to all documents emanating therefrom ; and shall perform such other duties as may be required of him by the Commandery or Commander.

XXVII.

Of Returns.

The returns of each Commandery shall be made up to the

first day of November, in each year, in such form as shall be prescribed by the Grand Commandery ; and shall immediately be forwarded to the Grand Recorder with the dues as hereinbefore provided.

CAAPTER IV.

MISCELLANEOUS.

XXVIII.

Of Trials and Appeals.

The mode of proceeding in all trials shall, as nearly as may be, be that which is now or may hereafter be prescribed in the Regulations of the Grand Lodge of Free and Accepted Masons of this State ; and appeals from the results of such trials may, in like manner as is directed by the Grand Lodge, be made to and adjudicated by the Grand Commandery.

XXIX.

Of Penalties.

Censure, suspension, or expulsion may be inflicted by any Commandery upon any Knight within its jurisdiction, for unknightly conduct or for violation of, or disobedience to any of the By-Laws, Statutes, Orders, Regulations, or Constitutions of the Order. Information of a suspension or expulsion by any Commandery, shall immediately be communicated by its Recorder, to the Recorder of each other Commandery in the State, and to the Grand Recorder ; but no publication thereof shall be made except by the Grand Commandery. Suspension may be removed by the Commandery which imposed it, but an expelled Knight can only be restored by the Grand Commandery.

4

XXX.

Of Vows of Office.

All officers of the Grand Commandery and of its subordinates, before entering upon the duties of their respective stations, shall take a solemn vow that they will maintain and support the Constitution and Regulations of the Grand Encampment of Knights Templar of the United States of America, and the Statutes and Orders of the Grand Commandery of the State of Alabama.

XXXI.

Of Amendments.

These Statutes may be altered or amended at any Annual Conclave, by the votes of two-thirds of the members present.

Form of Petition for a Dispensation.

TO OPEN AND HOLD A SUBORDINATE COMMANDERY.

To the Right Eminent Grand Commander
of Knights Templar in the State of Alabama:

The petition of the undersigned respectfully represents that they are severally Knights of the Red Cross, Knights Templar, and Knights of Malta; that they are now in good standing as Knights of those Illustrious, Valiant, and Magnanimous Orders, and were last members of the respective Commanderies named opposite their several signatures; that they reside in, or near the....................of..............in the county of......................in the State of Alabama; that among them are a competent number well qualified to form and open a Commandery of Knights Templar and the Appendant Orders, and to discharge the various duties thereof, according to ancient usage; and that, having the well-being and diffusion of Christian Chivalry at heart, and being desirous to extend its benefits and blessings to all worthy companions, they pray for a Dispensation empowering them to form, open, and hold a regular Commandery of Knights Templar and the Appendant Orders in the ....of.............. aforesaid, to be called ....Commandery. They beg leave respectfully to recommend Sir.................., as the first Commander, Sir......
........., as the first Generalissimo, and Sir ...., as the first Captain General; and, if their prayer be granted, they promise in all things to conform to the Statutes and Orders of the Grand Commandery of the State of Alabama, the Constitutions and Regulations of the Grand Encampment of the United States, and the general precepts and usages of the Order.

Dated at..........on the....... ..day of......... .A. D. 18...

(To the foregoing is to be appended the names of the petitioners, the names and numbers of the Commanderies of which they respectively last were members, and the State or Territory in which such Commanderies were holden.)

FORM OF APPLICATION FOR THE ORDERS OF KNIGHTHOOD.

*To the Eminent Commander, Generalissimo, Captain,
    General, and Knights of......... Commandery, No....*

The undersigned, respectfully represents that he has lawfully received the several degrees of Entered Apprentice, Fellow Craft, and Master Mason, in a regularly constituted Lodge, and of Mark Master, Past Master, Most Excellent Master, and the Royal Arch, in a regularly constituted Chapter ; that he is now in good standing, and is (or was late) a member of ....Chapter No......., in the ....of .... ; that he has resided in the State of Alabama, more than one year, and at the place below named more than three months next preceeding the date hereof ; that he has not, within twelve months past, been rejected by any Commandery of Knights Templar ; and that he is desirous of receiving the Orders of Knighthood conferred in your Commandery, and promises, if found worthy, to conform to all the ancient usages, and customs of the Order.

His place of residence is............, his age.........years, and his occupation,..................

    (Date.).........................., 18...

            (Signature.)................................

Recommended by

....
                        } *(To be members of the Commandery.)*
....

FORM OF APPLICATION FOR MEMBERSHIP IN A COMMANDERY.

To the Eminent Commander, Generalissimo, Captain
General, and Knights of............Commandery, No...

The undersigned, respectfully represents that he is a Knight of the Illustrious Order of the Red Cross, of the Valiant and Magnanimous Order of the Temple, and of the Order of Malta, or St. John of Jerusalem, in good standing ; that he was last a member of............... Commandery, No........., in the ....of..................., from which he has been honorably dismissed, as by the accompanying certificate will appear ; and that he now desires, if found worthy, to become a member of your Commandery.

His place of residence is..............., his age, ..., years, and his occupation ....

        (*Signature.*)...............................

(*Date.*)......... ...., 18...

Recommended by

...........................⎱
           ⎰ (*To be members of the Commandery.*)
....

Mobile Commandery, No. 2.

Mobile, Mobile County.

THE GENERAL GRAND ENCAMPMENT.

OF THE

United States of America.

To Whom it may Concern, Greeting:

W. B. HUBBARD,
G. G. Master.

WM. H. ELLIS,
D. G. G. Master.

CHAS. M. MOORE,
G. G. Generalissimo.

G. G. Capt. General.

Whereas, heretofore, to-wit: on the seventh day of April, in the year of our Lord, one thousand eight hundred and forty-eight, a *Dispensation* was granted to certain *Sir Knights* to open and hold an *Encampment of Knights Templar,* and the Appendant Order, in the City of Mobile, in the county of Mobile, and State of Alabama, by the name of Mobile Encampment, No. 2. *And whereas,* application has been made to this *General Grand Encampment,* for a perpetual *Charter* or *Warrant,* to enable them to continue in all the rights and privileges of a regularly *constituted Encampment,* and a copy of their *By-Laws,* and of the *Minutes* of their *Proceedings* having been submitted for *our* inspection and approval, and no cause adverse to the granting the prayer of said applicants to *us* appearing.

Now Know Ye, That *We The General Grand Encampment of the United States of America,* reposing special confidence and trust in the fidelity, zeal, and Masonic ability of the *Officers and Members* of the said *Encampment,* and for the purpose of diffusing the benefits of the *Order,* and promoting the happiness of man, by virtue of the power in *us* vested, *Do By These Presents,* recognise said *Encampment,* as regularly *constituted* and *established*, under the jurisdiction of this *General Grand Encampment*, with full and adequate powers to confer the several *Degrees of Knights of the Red Cross*, *Knights Templar*, and *Knights of Malta*, upon such person or persons, professing the requisite qualifications, as they may think proper. And *we*, do also recognise the present *Officers* and *Members* of the said *Encampment*, with continuance of the said powers and privileges, to them and their successors forever. *Provided*, *Nevertheless*, that the said *Officers* and *Members*, and their successors, pay due respect to *our* said *General Grand Encampment*, and to the *Constitution* and *Edicts* thereof, and in no way remove the Ancient *Land Marks* of *our Order;* *otherwise* this *Charter*, and all things therein contained, to be void, and of no effect.

[L. S.]

Given at the City of Washington, in the District of Columbia, this eighteenth day of March, in the year of our Lord, one thousand eight hundred and fifty-one, and of *our Order*, seven hundred and thirty-three.

By Order of the General Grand Encampment.

B. B. FRENCH,

G. G. Recorder.

OFFICERS OF THE PRESENT YEAR.

Sir John Johnson, E.: *Com.*, Sir Wm. Flash, *Treasurer*,
Sir Rich. F. Knott, *Gen'lissimo*,Sir Geo. W. Welch, *Re'er*,
Sir John H. Pippin, Capt. Gen.Sir Wm. Pick, *Stand. Bearer*,
Sir Wm. H. George, *Prelate*. Sir Lee Simpson, *Sword Bear.*
Sir Thos. Henry, *Sen. Warden*,Sir Thos. T. Tyree, *Warder*,
Sir O S. Beers, *Jun. Warden*,   Sir James C. Eastburn, *Sentinel*.

Past E.: Commmander:

Sir Charles W. Gazzam.

KNIGHTS NOW BORNE UPON THE ROLL.

Ayres, Sir Daniel, L.
Brown, Sir Peleg
Bowen, Sir John
Bythwood, Sir James G.
Brodenax, Sir Henry W.
Butt, Sir Cary W.
Barnard, Sir Francis J.
Calhoun, Sir J. C.
Carter, Sir Jesse
Cox, Sir Jesse J.
Cochran, Sir Samuel G.
Cox, Sir Benjamin B.
Clark, Sir Thomas J.
Cartright, Sir John
Davis, Sir D. R. W.
DeYampert, Sir Thomas J.
Douglass, Sir Leroy E.
Edwards, Sir Joseph R.
Fresinius, Sir John P.
Goodwin, Sir John W.

Hurtell, Sir John
Hurtell, Sir Firman
Harrison, Sir Richard K.
Hale, Sir Stephen F.
Hayes, Sir Charles
Hill, Sir James
Harper, Sir Martin B.
Johnson, Sir Charles B.
Marable, Sir C. C. M.
Means, Sir Hudson J.
McGuire, Sir Wesley W.
Oneal, Sir George W.
Prince, Sir John H.
Prince, Sir Edmund L.
Quigley, Sir Albert M.
Rawles, Sir John F.
Stone, Sir Sardine G.
Smaw, Sir Isaiah B.
Ulrick, Sir John G.
Welch, Sir William R.

Wilkins, Sir James.

Tuscumbia Commandery, No. 3,

Tuscumbia, Franklin County.

THE GENERAL GRAND ENCAMPMENT

OF THE

United States of America.

To whom it may concern, greeting:

W. B. HUBBARD,
G. G. Master.

WM. ELLIS,
D. G. G. Master.

CHAS. W. MOORE,
G. G. Generalissimo.

WM. F. GOULD,
G. G. Capt. General.

Whereas, heretofore, to-wit: On the 18th day of August, in the year of our Lord, one thousand eight hundred and forty-eight, a *Dispensation* was granted to certain *Sir Knights* to open and hold an *Encampment of Knights Templar*, and the appendant orders, in the City of Tuscumbia, in the county of Franklin, and State of Alabama, by the name of Tuscumbia Encampment, No. 3. *And whereas*, application has been made to this *General Grand Encampment*, for a perpetual *Charter* or *Warrant*, to enable them to continue in all the rights and privileges of a regularly *constituted Encampment*, and a copy of their *By-Laws*, and of the *Minutes* of their *Proceedings* having been submitted for *our* inspection and approval, and no cause adverse to granting the prayer of said applicants to *us* appearing:

Now know ye, that we, the General Grand Encampment of the United States of America, Reposing special confidence and trust in the fidelity, zeal, and Masonic ability of the *Officers* and *Members* of the said *Encampment*, and for the purpose of diffusing the benefits of the *Order*, and promoting the happiness of man, by virtue of the power in *us* vested, *Do by these*

5

Presents, recognise said *Encampment*, as regularly *Constituted* and *Established*, under the jurisdiction of this *General Grand Encampment*, with full and adequate powers to confer the several *Degrees* of *Knights of the Red Cross*, *Knights Templar*, and *Knights of Malta*, upon such person or persons, possessing the requisite qualifications, as they may think proper. And *we*, do also recognise the present *Officers* and *Members* of the said *Encampment*, with continuance of the said powers and privileges, to them and their *successors forever*. *Provided, nevertheless*, That the said *Officers* and *Members*, and their successors, pay due respect to *our* said *General Grand Encampment*, and to the *Constitution* and *Edicts* thereof, and in no way remove, the Ancient *Land Marks*, of *our Order: Otherwise* this *Charter*, and all things therein contained, to be void and of no effect.

[L. S.]

Given at the City of Washington, in the District of Columbia, this twelfth day of October, in the ;Year of Our Lord, One Thousand Eight Hundred and Fifty ; and of *Our Order*, Seven Hundred and Thirty-Two.

By order of the General Grand Encampment.

B. B. FRENCH,
G. G. Recorder.

OFFICERS FOR THE PRESENT YEAR.

Sir Anderson M. Barclay, E.'. Com., Sir William Simpson, Treasurer.
Sir Felix G. Norman, Generalissimo, Sir Lewis B. Thornton, Recorder,
Sir Charles A. Tony, Capt. General, Sir Alfred C. Matthews, St'd Bearer.
Sir Frederick A. Ross, Prelate,   Sir Stirling A. M. Wood, Sw'd Bearer.
Sir John Carey, Sen. Warden,   Sir Francis Moran, Warder,
Sir William M. Jackson, Jun. Wd'n, Sir Benjamin Pybas, Sentinel.

KNIGHTS NOW BORNE UPON THE ROLL :

Alexander, Sir Richard B.   Kimball, Sir Francis
Baker, Sir Joseph C.   Ladd, Sir Noble R.
Browning, Sir William H.   Lawson, Sir John
Bailey, Sir James J.   Lindsay, Sir David R.
Cannon, Sir David J.   Peet, Sir William A.
Carroll, Sir DeRosey   Perkins, Sir Thomas H.
Coffey, Sir William A.   Ragsdale, Sir J. B.
Chidester, Sir John T.   Rollston, Sir William
Early, Sir Thomas S.   Williams, Sir Charles
Harvey, Sir William   Williams, Sir Charles Foster,
Johnson, Sir Felix   Wood, Sir William B.

Vinson, Sir F. C.

Montgomery Commandery, No. 4.

Montgomery, Montgomery County.

THE GENERAL GRAND ENCAMPMENT OF KNIGHTS
TEMPLAR

OF THE

United States of America.

To whom it may concern, greeting:

W. B. HUBBARD,
G. G. Master.

WM. T. GOULD,
D. G. G. Master.

CHAS. W. MOORE,
G. G. Generalissimo.

E. S. BARNUM,
G. G. Capt. General.

Whereas, heretofore, to-wit: On the seventeenth day of October, in the year of our Lord, one thousand eight hundred and fifty, a *Dispensation* was granted to certain *Sir Knights* to open and hold an *Encampment of Knight's Templar*, and the appendant orders, in the City of Montgomery, in the county of Montgomery, and State of Alabama, by the name of Montgomery Encampment, No. 4. *And, whereas,* Application has been made to this *General Grand Encampment,* for a perpetual *Charter* or *Warrant,* to enable them to continue in all the rights and privileges of a regularly *Constituted Encampment,* and a copy of their *By-Laws,* and of the *Minutes* of their *Proceedings* having been submitted for *our* inspection and approval, and no cause adverse to the granting the prayer of said applicants to *us* appearing :

Now know ye, that we, the General Grand Encampment of the United States of America, Reposing special confidence and trust in the fidelity, zeal, and Masonic ability of the *Officers* and *Members* of the said *Encampment,* and for the purpose of diffusing the benefits of the *Order,* and promoting the happiness of man, by virtue of the power in *us* vested, *Do, by these presents*, recognise said *Encampment*, as regularly *Constituted* and *established*, under the jurisdiction of this *General Grand Encampment*, with full and adequate powers to confer the several *Degrees of Knights of the Red Cross*, *Knights Templar*, and *Knights of Malta*, upon such person or persons, possessing the requisite qualifications, as they may think proper. And *we*, do also recognise the present *Officers* and *Members* of the said *Encampment*, with continuance of the said powers and privileges, to them and their successors forever. *Provided, Nevertheless*, that the said *Officers* and *Members*, and their successors, pay due respect to *our* said *General Grand Encampment*, and to the *Constitution* and *Edicts* thereof, and in no way remove the Ancient *Land Marks* of our *Order ;* *otherwise* this *Charter*, and all things therein contained, to be void, and of no effect.

[L. S.]

Given at the City of Washington, in the District of Columbia, this nineteenth day of Sept., in the year of our Lord, one thousand eight hundred and fifty-three, and of *our Order*, seven hundred and thirty-five.

By Order of the General Grand Encampment.

B. B. FRENCH,
G. G. Recorder.

OFFICERS OF THE PRESENT YEAR.

Sir Hugh P. Watson, E.·. Commander, Sir Benjamin S. Thiess, Treasurer.
Sir Henry P. Lee, Generalissimo, Sir Richard Fraser, Recorder,
Sir Abram J. Walker, Capt. General, Sir John P. Dickinson, St'd Bearer,
Sir Edmund M. Hastings, Prelate, Sir Noah B. Cloud, Sword Bearer,
Sir B. Massie, Sen. Warden, Sir Joseph M. Williams, Warder,
Sir William G. Andrews, Jun. Warden, Sir Thomas McDougal, Sentinel.

Past E.: Commander:

Sir Samuel B. Marks.

KNIGHTS NOW BORNE UPON THE ROLL.

Bibb, Sir William C.
Bowen, Sir James, H.
Chilton, Sir William P.
Danforth, Sir Joshua H.
Dixon, Sir Samuel H.
Dorman, Sir Thomas W.
Fariss, Sir William B.
Figh, Sir John P.
Figh Sir George M.
Gunter, Sir Charles G.
Harrison, Sir Edmund,
Jones, Sir George
Judge, Sir Thomas J.
Morgan, Sir John T.
Mathews, Sir George H. B.
Mathews, Sir George W.
Mathews, Sir William B.
Mathews, Sir Samuel B.
Mathews, Sir Francis M.
Martin, Sir James B.
McCall, Sir D. A.
McSpadden, Sir S. K.
Norton, Sir Samuel E.
Parsons, Sir Lewis E.
Shelton, Sir Humphrey S.
Stewart, Sir Edward S.
Watson, Sir Samuel D.
Welsh, Sir Thomas
Willoughby, Sir John H.

Selma Commandery, No. 5.

Selma, Dallas County.

THE GRAND ENCAMPMENT OF KNIGHTS TEMPLAR.

OF THE

United States of America.

To Whom it may Concern, Greeting:

W. B. HUBBARD,
G. Master of Knights Templar.

D. G. Master.

D. S. GOODLOE,
G. Generalissimo.

G. Capt. General.

Whereas, heretofore, to-wit: on the thirteenth day of May, in the year of our Lord, one thousand eight hundred and fifty-eight, a *Dispensation* was granted to certain *Sir Knights* to open and hold a *Commandery of Knights Templar,* and the Appendant Orders, in the City of Selma, in the county of Dallas, and State of Alabama, by the name of Selma Commandery, No. 5. *And whereas,* application has been made to this *Grand Encampment,* for a perpetual *Charter* or *Warrant,* to enable them to continue in all the rights and privileges of a regularly *constituted Commandery,* and a copy of their *By-Laws,* and of the *Minutes* of their *Proceedings* having been submitted for *our* inspection and approval, and no cause adverse to the granting of the prayer of said applicants to *us* appearing.

Now know ye, That *we, the Grand Encampment of Knights Templar of the United States of America,* reposing special confidence and trust in the fidelity, zeal, and Masonic ability of the *Officers and Members* of the said *Commandery,* and for the purpose of diffusing the benefits of the *Order,* and promoting the happiness of man, by virtue of the power in *us* vested, *Do By These Presents,* recognise said *Commandery,* as regularly *constituted* and *established*, under the jurisdiction of this Grand Encamment, with full and adequate powers to confer the several *Degrees of Knights of the Red Cross* and *Knights Templar*, upon such person or persons, possessing the necessary qualifications, as they may think proper, and to instruct them, as to the legend and qualifications of *Knights of Malta*. And *we* do also recognise the present *Officers* and *Members* of said *Commandery*, with continuance of the said powers and privileges, to them and their *successors forever*, except that the officers of said Commandery, shall not be entitled to act as members of *Our Grand Encampment*, until they are duly elected and installed, under this *Charter*. *Provided, nevertheless*, That the said *Officers* and *Members*, and their successors, pay due respect to *our* said *Grand Encampment*, and to the *Constitution* and *Edicts* thereof, and in no way remove the ancient *Land Marks* of *Our Order: Otherwise* this *Charter*, and all things therein contained, to be void and of no effect.

[L. S.]

Given at the City of Chicago, in the State of Illinois, this sixteenth day of Sept., in the year of our Lord, one thousand eight hundred and fifty-nine, and of our Order, seven hundred and forty-one. *By Order of the Grand Encampment of Knights Templar of the United States.*

B. B. FRENCH,

G. Recorder.

OFFICERS FOR THE PRESENT YEAR.

Sir **James B.** Harrison, E.·. Com., Sir Jacob Krout, Treasurer,
Sir **Andrew J.** Goodwin, Genl'mo, Sir Richard Faxon, Recorder,
Sir **William S.** Knox, Capt. General, Sir Henry Traun, Standard Bearer,
Sir **Benjamin J.** Harrison, Prelate, Sir J. A. Mimms, Sword Bearer,
Sir **George F.** Plant, Sen. Warden, Sir John M. Strong, Warder,
Sir **John Riggs**, Jun. Warden, Sir William Hardy, Sentinel.

KNIGHTS NOW BORNE UPON THE ROLL.

W. H. Tarrance.

(N. B.—No returns have been received from Washington Commandery,
No. 1. E. M. H., G. Recorder.)

Committee on Foreign Correspondence.

Sir Abram J. Walker, Montgomery, Montgomery County,
Sir Lewis B. Thornton, Tuscumbia, Franklin County,
Sir Porter King, Marion, Perry County,
Sir Peleg Brown, Mobile, Mobile County,
Sir Benjamin J. Harrison, Selma, Dallas County.

FORM OF RETURN TO THE GRAND COMMANDERY.

Annual Return of......... Commandery No. ......, to the Grand Commandery of the State of Alabama.

Number of members.	Names.	Grade.	Date of Red Cross.	Date of Knighting.	Dues.	Dead or withdrawn	Suspended or expelled
1	....	E. C.	....	....			....
2	....	G.	....	....		Died.	*Suspended.*
3	....	C. G.	....	....		E F 11 J. '61	J. K. 1 F. '61
4	....	Pre'te	....	....			....
5	....	S. W	....	....		....	....
6	....	J. W.	....	....		....	....
7	....	Treas.	....	....		Withd'wn.	*Expelled.*
8	....	Rec.	....	....		G. H........	None.
9	....	Std.B.	....	....		....	....
10	....	Swd B	....	....		....	....
11	....	Wd'er	....	....		....	....
12	....	Sent.	....	....		....	....
13	....	P E C	....	....		....	....
14	A. B........	K. T.	12. Jan. '61.	12 Jan. '61.		....	....
15	C. D........	" "	15. Feb. "	20 M'ch "	S		....

I..........., Commander of..........., Commandery No......., do certify that the above is a correct annual return of said Commandery held in the........., of........., in the county of ...., from the......... day of........., 18... to the 1st day of November, 18...

In Testimony, Whereof, I have hereunto set my
L. S.   hand and caused to be affixed the Seal of said Commandery this..........day of..........., A. D. 18...
A. O. 74...

Attest.   J. B. H.......   R. F. K....
       RECORDER,   E. COMMANDER.

REGISTER OF GRAND COMMANDERIES,
UNDER THE JURISDICTION OF THE GRAND ENCAMPMENT OF THE UNITED STATES.

Grand Commanderies.	Grand Commanders.	Residences.	Grand Recorders.	Residences.	No. of Commanderies.	No. of Knights.	Formed.
Alabama,	Richard F. Knott,	Mobile,	Edmund M. Hastings	Montgomery,	5	144	December 1, 1860
California,	Leander Ranson,	S. Francisco,	Alexander G. Abell,	San Francisco,	6	204	August 10, 1858.
Connecticut,	George F. Daskam,	Norwalk,	Eliphalet G. Story,	New Haven,	6	396	Betw'n '29 & '32.
Illinois,	J. V. Z. Blaney,	Chicago,	William H. Turner,	Alton,	5	222	Oct. 27, 1857.
Indiana,	George W. Porter,	New Albany,	Francis King,	Indianapolis,	7	223	May 16, 1854.
Kentucky,	S. F. Gano,	Georgetown,	Wm. M. Samuels,	Paris,	10	210	Betw'n '47 & '50.
Maine,	Freeman Bradford,	Portland,	Ira Berry,	Portland,	4	141	May 5, 1852.
Mass & Rhode Island	Winslow Lewis,	Boston,	Wm. H. L. Smith,	Boston,	9	613	Prior to 1819.
Michigan,	Nathaniel P. Jacobs,	Detroit,	George W. Wilson,	Ionia,	5	*300	April 7, 1857.
Mississippi,	Giles M. Hillyer,	Natchez,	Rt. W. T. Daniel,	Jackson,	5	216	January 22, 1857.
Missouri,	George W. Belt,	Weston,	Edward G. Heriot,	Weston,	4	201	Prior to 1826.
New York,	Charles G. Judd,	Penn Yan,	Robert Macoy,	New York,	23	1062	May 24, 1860.
Ohio,	John H. Achey,	Dayton,	John D. Caldwell,	Cincinnati,	15	*800	Prior to 1819.
Pennsylvania,	Wm. H. Allen, L.L.D	Philadelphia	Alfred Creigh,	Washington,	19	500	October 1843.
Tennessee,	Charles A. Fuller,	Nashville,	William H. Whitton,	Columbia,	4	165	April 12, 1854.
Texas,	George M. Patrick,	Anderson,	Andrew Neill,	Seguin,	6	270	October 12, 1859.
Vermont,	Barzillai Davenport,	Brandon,	John B. Hollenbeck,	Burlington,	4	178	January 19, 1855.
Virginia,	E H. Gill,	Richmond,	John Dove,	Richmond,	10	408	August 11, 1851.
Total					147	Total...6252	

*Number of Members estimated.

SUBORDINATE COMMANDERIES,

UNDER THE JURISDICTION OF THE GRAND COMMANDERY OF THE STATE OF ALABAMA.

Commanderies.	Nos.	Places.	County.	Commanders.	Recorders.	No. of Knights.	Date of Charter.
Washington	1	Marion	Perry	Sir	Sir	......	No return.
Mobile	2	Mobile	Mobile	Sir John Johnson	Sir George W. Welch	54	March 18, 1851.
Tuscumbia	3	Tuscumbia	Franklin	Sir Anderson M. Barclay	Sir Lewis B. Thornton	35	October 12, 1850.
Montgomery	4	Montgomery	Montgomery	Sir Hugh P. Watson	Sir Richard Fraser	42	Sept. 19, 1853.
Selma	5	Selma	Dallas	Sir James B. Harrison	Sir Richard Faxon	13	Sept. 16, 1859.
					Total	144	

OFFICERS

OF THE

GRAND ENCAMPMENT OF THE UNITED STATES,

ELECTED SEPTEMBER, A. D., 1859, A. O., 741.

M∴ E∴ Benjamin B. French, Grand Master, Washington, D. C.,

R∴ E∴ David S. Goodloe, Deputy Grand Master, Lexington, Ky.,

V∴ E∴ Winslow Lewis, Grand Generalissimo, Boston, Mass.,

" " James V. Z. Blaney, Grand Captain General, Chicago, Ill.,

" " Charles Marsh, Grand Senior Warden, Nevada, California.

" " Azariah T. C. Pierson, Grand Junior Warden, St. Paul, Min.,

" " John W. Simons, Grand Treasurer, New York City,

" " Samuel G. Risk, Grand Recorder, New Orleans, La.,

" " Abner B. Thompson, Grand Standard Bearer, Brunswick, Me.,

" " Robert M. Henderson, Grand Sword Bearer, Lexington, Mo.,

" " Nathaniel P. Jacobs, Grand Warder, Detroit, Mich.

OFFICERS

OF THE

GRAND COMMANDERY OF ALABAMA,

ELECTED DECEMBER, A. D., 1860, A. O., 742.

R∴ E∴ Richard F. Knott, Grand Commander, Mobile,

V∴ E∴ Sterling A. M. Wood, Deputy Grand Commander, Florence,

E∴ James B. Harrison, Grand Generalissimo, Selma,

" Peleg Brown, Grand Captain General, Mobile.

" Henry Talbird, Grand Prelate, Marion,

" Porter King, Grand Senior Warden, Marion,

" Lewis B. Thornton, Grand Junior Warden, Tuscumbia,

" Hugh P. Watson, Grand Treasurer, Montgomery,

" Edmund M. Hastings, Grand Recorder, Montgomery,

" John H. Pippin, Grand Standard Bearer, Mobile,

,, William S. Knox, Grand Sword Bearer, Selma,

" Joseph M. Williams, Grand Warder, Montgomery.

" Joseph McGaw, Grand Sentinel, Mobile.

CONSTITUTION

OF THE

Grand Encampment of Knights Templar

FOR THE

UNITED STATES OF AMERICA,

As Amended at the Triennial Meeting begun and held in the City of Chicago, Illinois, on Tuesday, September 13, 1859, and the Year of the Order 741.

ARTICLE FIRST,

Of the Grand Encampment of the United States.

SECTION 1.—How Constituted.

The Grand Encampment of Knights Templar of the United
States, is constituted as follows:

    I. The Grand Master.

    II. The Deputy Grand Master.

    III. The Grand Generalissimo.

    IV. The Grand Captain General.

    V. The Grand Prelate.

    VI. The Grand Senior Warden.

    VII. The Grand Junior Warden.

    VIII. The Grand Treasurer.

    IX. The Grand Recorder.
    X. The Grand Standard Bearer.
    XI. The Grand Sword Bearer.
    XII. The Grand Warder.
    XIII. The Grand Captain of the Guards.

LIKEWISE.

    XIV. All Past Grand Masters.
    XV. All Past Deputy Grand Masters.
    XVI. All Past Grand Generalissimos, and
    XVII. All Past Grand Captains General of the Grand Encampment of the United States.

LIKEWISE.

    XVIII. All Grand Commanders.
    XIX. All Past Grand Commanders.
    XX. All Deputy Grand Commanders.
    XXI. All Grand Generalissimos, and
    XXII. All Grand Captains General of each State Grand Commandery that acknowledges the jurisdiction of the United States Grand Encampment.

Each of the individuals above enumerated shall be entitled, when present, to one vote in all the proceedings of the Grand Encampment of the United States.

LIKEWISE.

    XXIII. The first three officers of each Commandery that holds its charter immediately from the Grand Encampment of the United States.

These, or as many of them as may be present at any meeting of the Grand Encampment of the United States, shall be entitled collectively to one vote.

All officers of the late General Grand Encampment shall rank and have all the privileges of members of equal rank as provided for herein.

No person shall be eligible to any office in the Grand Encampment of the United States, unless he shall be at the time a member of some Subordinate Commandery under the general or immediate jurisdiction of the Grand Encampment of the United States.

SECTION 2.—PROXIES.

The first four officers named in Section 1, of this Article, likewise the first four officers of all State Grand Commanderies; likewise the first three officers of all Subordinate Chartered Commanderies held under the immediate jurisdiction of the Grand Encampment of the United States, may appear and vote *by proxy;* said proxies being at the time of service members of Subordinate Commanderies, and producing properly authenticated certificates of their appointment.

SECTION 3.—TITLES.

The title and designation of the Grand Master of the Grand Encampment of the United States, is *Most Eminent Grand Master of Knights Templar;* that of the Deputy Grand Master, *Right Eminent;* of the remaining officers of the Grand Encampment, *Very Eminent.*

SECTION 4.—MEETINGS.

The stated meetings of the Grand Encampment of the United States shall occur triennially on the *First Tuesday of September*, at such places as may have been previously designated by the Standing Committee (see Art. IV, Sec. 4, Rule 4,) and approved by the Grand Encampment of the United States.

Special meetings may be called by the Most Eminent Grand Master at his discretion. And it shall be his duty, upon the requisition of the majority of the State Grand Commanderies, to him directed in writing, to call special meetings of the Grand Encampment of the United States.

The Grand Officers shall hold their respective offices until their successors shall be duly elected and installed.

At the stated meetings of the Grand Encampment of the United States, there shall be reviewed and considered all the official reports of its officers, and of the State Grand and Sub-ordinate Commanderies, for the preceding three years ; they shall proceed to elect by ballot the several officers of the Grand Encampment of the United States, save and except the Pre-late and Captain of the Guards, who shall be appointed by the Grand Master at the opening of the triennial sessions (see Art. 1, Sec. 5 ;) to adopt such rules and edicts as may be necessa-ry for the good of the Order ; to examine the accounts of the Grand Treasurer and Grand Recorder ; to supervise the state and condition of the finances, and adopt such measures in re-lation thereto as may be necessary to increase, secure and pre-serve the same, and also to insure the utmost punctuality on the part of every accounting officer in the safe keeping and paying over the funds and property of the Grand Encamp-ment ; to grant or withhold warrants, dispensations and char-ters for all new State or Subordinate Commanderies, (see Art. II, Sec. 1, and Art. III, Sec. 1 ;) for good cause to revoke pre-existing warrants, charters or dispensations ; to assign the limits of the State Grand Commanderies, and settle all con-troversies that may arise between them ; and finally, to con-sider and do all matters and things appertaining to the good, well-being and perpetuation of the principles of Templar Ma-sonry.

No business shall be transacted at the called meetings, save that which was specified in the original summons.

At every meeting, all questions shall be determined by a majority of votes, the presiding officer being entitled to one vote. In case the votes are equally divided, he has the cast-ing vote. This Grand Encampment being a legislative body, acknowledging no superior, admits an appeal to be taken by any member from the decision of the chair on any question un-der consideration therein. Provided, however, that such ap-peal shall not be maintained unless two-thirds of all the mem-bers present shall vote therefor. That right is adopted for this Grand Encampment alone, and is not to be construed as establishing a precedent for the guidance of any other Masonic Body.

SECTION 5.—Duties of the Officers.

I. The Grand Master.

It is the prerogative and duty of the Grand Master, generally to exercise, as occasion may require, all the rights appertaining to his high office, in accordance with the usages of Templar Masonry. And as a part thereof, he shall have a watchful supervision over all the Commanderies, State and Subordinate, in the United States, and see that all the constitutional enactments, rules and edicts of the Grand Encampment are duly and promptly observed, and that the dress, work and discipline of Templar Masonry everywhere are uniform.

Among his special duties and prerogatives are the following :

To appoint the Prelate and Captain of the Guard, at the triennial meetings of the Grand Encampment. (See Art. 1, Sec. 4.)

To call special meetings of the Grand Encampment of the United States. (Art. 1, Sec. 4.)

To visit and preside at any Commandery, Grand or Subordinate, in the United States, and give such instructions and directions as the good of the Institution may require, always adhering to the Ancient Landmarks.

To cause to be executed, and securely to preserve and keep, the official bonds and securities of the Grand Treasurer and Grand Recorder. (See Art. IV, Sec. 3.)

To grant Letters of Dispensation during the recess of the Grand Encampment, for the institution of new Commanderies (see Art. III, Sec. 1 ;) such Dispensations to be in force no longer than the next triennial meeting of that body, and promptly to notify the Grand Recorder of the issuing of said Letters of Dispensation.

To approve and grant Warrants during the recess of the Grand Encampment for the institution of State Grand Commanderies in States, Districts or Territories where the same have not been heretofore established. (See Art. II, Sec. 1.)

To manage and control the contingent fund. (See Art. IV, Sec. 1.)

2. The Deputy Grand Master..

The Deputy Grand Master, in the event of the death, removal, or physical incompetency of his superior, shall act as the Grand Master. At all other times he shall perform such duties as may be assigned him by the Grand Encampment or the Grand Master.

3. The Grand Generalissimo and Grand Captain General.

In the absence of their respective superiors, the Grand Generalissimo and Grand Captain General shall severally act as Grand Master, in order, according to rank. At all other times they shall perform such duties as may be assigned them by the Grand Encampment, or such as are traditionally appropriate to their respective stations.

4. The Grand Treasurer.

The Grand Treasurer, unless otherwise directed by the Grand Encampment, shall invest from time to time, all such moneys as may come to his hands belonging to the Grand Encampment, over and above the sum of three hundred dollars, in such way as he may judge most to the interest of the Grand Encampment, but subject to call on thirty days' notice. And the same shall be at his command on the first day of September preceding the triennial meeting of the Grand Encampment. He shall render to the Grand Encampment at its triennial meetings, a true and perfect account of his doings in this respect, together with an account of all moneys received, the earnings thereon accrued from investments, and the amounts disbursed by him during the vacation ; likewise a copy of the same to the Grand Master, by the first day of September preceding the triennial meeting, to the end that the Grand Master may make such suggestions on account thereof as he may deem necessary.

He shall pay all drafts drawn upon the contingent fund by the Grand Master. (See Art. IV, Sec. 1.)

He shall carefully preserve and render from time to time as ordered, an inventory of all property belonging to the Grand Encampment entrusted to his keeping.

5. The Grand Recorder.

The Grand Recorder shall collect and receive all the revenues of the Grand Encampment, and pay over the amount to the Grand Treasurer whenever it reaches the sum of one hundred dollars. He shall render annually to the Grand Master and to the Grand Treasurer copies of his accounts of all moneys received and expended by him—naming the sources from which they were received—bringing up said accounts to the first day of September ; likewise to the Grand Encampment, triennially, a general account of the same. He shall forward to each newly constituted Commandery, immediately upon receiving official notice that a Dispensation has issued, a copy of this Constitution. together with whatever rules and edicts are in force.

He shall report to the Grand Encampment on the second day of each triennial meeting, the names of those Commanderies working under the immediate jurisdiction of the Grand Encampment, which have not complied with the requisition, (see Art. III, Sec. 4,) to furnish him with its full triennial historical and financial returns for the use of the Grand Encampment.

He shall report annually on the first day of September to the Grand Master the names of those Commanderies working under the immediate jurisdiction of the Grand Encampment which have not complied with the requisition (see Art. III, Sec. 4,) to furnish him with its full annual historical and financial returns for the use of the Grand Master.

He shall open and keep a "Book of Templar Masonry," in which shall be entered in appropriate columns the following subjects :

A.—A Register of Commanderies, to contain,

1. The date of issuing of every Warrant, Dispensation and Charter for a Grand or Subordinate Commandery, granted by authority of the Grand Encampment since its origin.

2. The roll of officers of the Grand Conclave of the Royal, Exalted, Religious and Military Order of Masonic Knights Templar in England and Wales, together with the roll of Encampments, officers and members of the Provincial Grand Conclave of Canada.

B.—A Register of Membership, to contain,

1. The roll of officers of the Grand Encampment, with their terms of service, etc., etc., since the origin of the same.

2. The roll of officers and members of each Grand and Subordinate Commandery now working under the jurisdiction of the Grand Encampment, with all the current changes resulting from removals, dismissions, suspensions, expulsions and deaths.

C.—Historical Data, tending to lighten up the history of Templar Masonry in the United States.

Likewise, to collect and in orderly volumes bind a copy of all the proceedings of the Grand Encampment since its organization, together with copies of by-laws, impressions of seals, proceedings of State Grand Commanderies, etc., etc., and to make a triennial report of his official acts.

G. The Remaining Officers.

The duties of the remaining officers of the Grand Encampment are such as are traditionally appropriate to their respective stations, or such as may be assigned them by the Grand Encampment.

The Grand Master, the Deputy Grand Master, the Grand Generalissimo, and the Grand Captain General, are severally authorized to visit and preside in any Commandery of Knights Templar throughout the jurisdiction of the Grand Encampment, and to give such instructions and directions as the good of the institution may require, always adhering to the ancient landmarks.

In the event of the absence of all the four principal officers of the Grand Encampment, the Past Grand Officers, according to rank and seniority of service shall be empowered to preside.

The Grand Treasurer and Grand Recorder shall severally give bond and security, in such form and to such an amount —but not less than double the estimated triennial receipts by either—as shall from time to time be determined by the Grand Master, who shall judge and approve of the sufficiency of such bonds and securities, and who shall keep and preserve the same.

Any Grand officer—save as above excepted—coming into the receipt of moneys or property belonging to the Grand Encampment, shall forthwith remit the same to the Grand Recorder.

ARTICLE SECOND,

Of the State Grand Commanderies.

SECTION 1.—How Constituted.

Whenever there shall be three or more Subordinate Chartered Commanderies instituted or holden under this Constitution, in any one State, District or Territory, in which a Grand Encampment has not been heretofore formed, a *Grand Commandery* may be formed after obtaining the approval of the Grand Master or the Grand Encampment. Its jurisdiction shall be the territorial limits in which it is holden.

A State Grand Commandery consists of the following members :

    I. The Grand Commander.
    II. The Deputy Grand Commander.
    III. The Grand Generalissimo.
    IV. The Grand Captain General.
    V. The Grand Prelate.
    VI. The Grand Senior Warden.
    VII. The Grand Junior Warden.
    VIII. The Grand Treasurer.
    IX. The Grand Recorder.
    X. The Grand Standard Bearer.
    XI. The Grand Sword Bearer.
    XII. The Grand Warder.
    XIII. The Grand Captain of the Guards.

LIKEWISE.

XIV. All Past Grand Commanders [and Grand Masters.]

XV. All Past Deputy Grand Commanders [and Deputy Grand Masters.]

XVI. All Past Grand Generalissimos, and

XVII. All Past Grand Captains General of the same Grand Commandery so long as they remain members of the Subordinate Commanderies under the same territorial jurisdiction.

XVIII. The Commander
XIX. The Generalissimos, and
XX. The Captain General of each Subordinate Commandery, working under the same Grand Commandery.

XXI. All Past Commanders of the Subordinate Commanderies working under the same Grand Commanderies so long as they remain members of Subordinate Commanderies under the same territorial jurisdiction.

Each of the individuals enumerated shall be entitled, when present, to one vote in all the proceedings of the State Grand Commandery.

No person shall be eligible to any office in the State Grand Commandery unless he shall be at the time a member of some Subordinate Commandery working under the same Grand Commandery.

The Grand Commandery of Massachusetts and Rhode Island is recognized as holding jurisdiction over both those States.

SECTION 2.—PROXIES.

Any officer specified in Section 1st of this Article, save and except Past Commanders, may appear and vote *by proxy*, said proxy being at the time of service a member of the same Subordinate Commandery as his principal, and producing a properly authenticated certificate of his appointment.

SECTION 3.—TITLES.

The title and designation of the Grand Commander of a State Grand Commandery is *Right Eminent;* that of Deputy Grand Commander, *Very Eminent:* of the remaining officers of the Grand Commandery, *Eminent.*

SECTION 4.—MEETINGS.

The stated meetings of a State Grand Commandery shall occur annually, at such time and place as said Grand Commandery in its discretion may direct.

Special meetings may be called by the Grand Commander at his discretion.

The several Grand Officers shall hold their respective offices until their successors shall be duly elected and installed.

At the stated meetings of each Grand Commandery, there shall be reviewed and considered all the official reports of its officers, and of the Subordinate Commanderies, within its jurisdiction for the preceding year. They shall proceed to elect by ballot the several officers of the Grand Commandery (see Art. II, Sec. 1.) To adopt such rules and edicts, subordinate to the Constitution of the Grand Encampment of the United States, as may be necessary for the good of the Order. To examine the accounts of the Grand Treasurer and Grand Recorder. To supervise the state and condition of the finances, and adopt such measures in relation thereto as may be necessary to increase, secure and preserve the same, and also to insure the utmost punctuality on the part of every accounting officer in the safe keeping and paying over the funds and property of the Grand Commandery. To grant or withhold Dispensations and Charters for all new Commanderies. For good cause to revoke any pre-existing Charter or Dispensation ; to assign the limits of Subordinate Commanderies within its own jurisdiction, and settle all controversies that may arise between them ; and finally, to consider and do all matters and things appertaining to the good, well-being and perpetuation of Templar Maosnry, but always subordinate to the Grand Encampment of the United States.

No business shall be transacted at the *called* meetings, save that which was specified in the original summons.

At every meeting, all questions shall be determined by a majority of votes, the presiding officer being entitled to one vote. In case the votes are equally divided, he shall also give the casting vote. No appeal shall lie to the Grand Commandery from the decision of the Grand Commander.

SECTION 5.—DUTIES OF THE OFFICERS.

1. The Grand Commander.

The Grand Commander of a State Grand Commandery shall have a watchful supervision over all the Subordinate Commanderies under his jurisdiction, and see that all the constitutional enactments, rules and edicts of the Grand Encampment of the United States, and of his own Grand Commandery, are duly and promptly observed.

He shall have the power and authority, during the recess of his Grand Commandery, to grant Letters of Dispensation to a competent number of petitioners, nine or more, residing within his jurisdiction, and possessing the constitutional qualifications empowering them to form and open a Commandery ; such Dispensations to be in force no longer than the next annual meeting of his Grand Commandery. But no Letters of Dispensation for constituting a new Commandery shall be issued, save upon the recommendation of the Commandery in the same territorial jurisdiction nearest the place of the new Commandery prayed for.

He may call special meetings of his Grand Commandery at his discretion. (See Art. II, Sec. 4.)

He may visit and preside at any Commandery within the jurisdiction of his Grand Commandery, and give such instructions and directions as the good of the institution may require, but always adhering to the ancient landmarks.

It is his duty, either in person or by proxy, to attend all meetings of the Grand Encampment of the United States.

2. The Deputy Grand Commander.

The Deputy Grand Commander, in the event of the death, removal, or physical incompetency of his superior, shall act as the Grand Commander. At all other times he shall perform such duties as may be assigned him by the Commandery or the Grand Commander.

It is his duty, either in person or by proxy, to attend all meetings of the Grand Encampment of the United States.

3. The Grand Generalissimo and Grand Captain General.

In the absence of their respective superiors, the Grand Generalissimo and Grand Captain General shall severally act as Grand Commanders, in order, according to rank. At all other times they shall perform such duties as may be assigned them by the Grand Commandery, or such as are traditionally appropriate to their respective stations.

It is their duty, either in person or by proxy, to attend all meetings of the Grand Encampment of the United States.

4. The Grand Recorder.

The Grand Recorder shall make an annual communication to the Grand Recorder of each of the other Grand Commanderies, likewise to the Grand Master and Grand Recorder of the Grand Encampment of the United States ; said communication to embrace the roll of Grand Officers, and such other matters as may conduce to the general good of the Order. He shall also regularly transmit to the Grand Master and Grand Recorder of the Grand Encampment of the United States copies of the By-Laws and Regulations adopted by his Grand Commandery.

The duties of the remaining officers, as well as of those above specified, shall be such as are traditionally appropriate to their respective stations, or allotted to them by the Grand Commandery, and corresponding as near as may be to those of the corresponding officers of the Grand Encampment of the United States.

In the event of the absence of all the four principal officers of the Grand Commandery, the Past Grand Officers, according to the rank and seniority of service, shall be empowered to preside.

ARTICLE THIRD,

Of Subordinate Commanderies.

SECTION 1.—How Constituted.

Each State Grand Commandery shall have exclusive power *to constitute new Commanderies* within its jurisdiction. During the recess of the Grand Commandery, the Grand Commander shall have the power to grant *Letters of Dispensation* to a competent number of petitioners, nine or more, possessing the constitutional qualifications, and residing within its territorial jurisdiction, empowering them to form and open a Commandery for a term of time not extending beyond the next stated meeting of the Grand Commandery.

The Grand Encampment of the United States shall have exclusive power to constitute new Commanderies within any State, District or Territory, wherein there is no State Commandery regularly formed under the authority of the Grand Encampment of the United States. During the recess of the

Grand Encampment the Grand Master shall have the power to grant Letters of Dispensation to a competent number of petitioners, nine or more, possessing the constitutional qualifications, and residing within said unappropriated State, District or Territory, empowering them to form and open a Commandery for a term of time, not extending beyond the next stated meeting of the Grand Encampment of the United States.

A Subordinate Commandery consists of the following members :

      I. The Commander.
     II. The Generalissimo.
    III. The Captain General.
    IV. The Prelate.
     V. The Senior Warden.
    VI. The Junior Warden.
   VII. The Treasurer.
  VIII. The Recorder.
    IX. The Standard Bearer.
     X. The Sword Bearer.
    XI. The Warder.

LIKEWISE.

    XII. As many members as may be found convenient for work and discipline.

Each of the individuals enumerated in this section shall be entitled, when present, to one vote in all the proceedings of the Subordinate Commandery.

SECTION 2.—TITLES.

The title and designation of the Commander of a Subordinate Commandery, is *Eminent*.

SECTION 3.—MEETINGS.

The stated meetings of a Subordinate Commandery shall occur at least semi-annually, at such time and place as may be specified in the Charter, or designated in the By-Laws of the Commandery.

Special meetings may be called by the Commander at his discretion.

The several officers shall hold their respective offices until their successors be duly elected and installed.

No business shall be performed at the *called* meetings, save that which was specified in the original summons.

At every meeting, all questions shall be determined by a majority of votes, the presiding officer for the time being, being entitled to one vote. In case the votes are equally divided, he shall also give the casting vote. No appeal shall lie to the Subordinate Commandery, from the decision of the Commander.

SECTION 4.—DUTIES OF THE OFFICERS.

The Commander.

The Commander has it in special charge to see that the By-Laws of his Commandery are duly observed, as well as the Constitution, Rules and Edicts of the State Grand Commandery, and of the Grand Encampment of the United States; that accurate records are kept and just accounts rendered; that regular returns are made to the Grand Encampment or Commandery, annually; and that the annual dues are promptly paid.

It is his duty, together with the Generalissimo and Captain General, either in person or proxy, to attend all meetings of his Grand Encampment, or Commandery.

The Recorder.

It shall be the duty of the Recorder of every Subordinate Commandery, working under the immediate jurisdiction of the Grand Encampment of the United States, to report annually to the Grand Recorder of the Grand Encampment of the United States, up to the first day of August, the roll of his officers and members, and the working roll of his Commandery ; and to accompany the same with the amount of dues to the Grand Encampment of the United States. For failure herein, the Commandery so offending, shall be subject to Knightly discipline.

In the event of the absence of all the three principal officers of the Commandery, the Past Commanders, according to rank and seniority of service, shall be empowered to preside.

ARTICLE FOURTH,

Miscellaneous.

SECTION 1.—FEES, DUES, AND FINANCIALS.

The fee for instituting a new Commandery shall be not less than ninety dollars.

For every Knight Templar created in any Commandery, holden by Dispensation or Charter whilst under the immediate jurisdiction of the Grand Encampment of the United States, there shall be paid two dollars into the Treasury of the Grand Encampment of the United States.

The Grand Recorder of the Grand Encampment of the United States shall receive ten dollars as his fee for each Charter issued, and five dollars for endorsing, under the seal of the Grand Encampment of the United States, the extension of a Dispensation.

The State Grand Commanderies, respectively, shall possess authority, upon the institution of new Commanderies within their respective jurisdiction, to require from the several Commanderies within their respective jurisdiction, such proportions of the sums received by them for conferring the Orders ; likewise, such sums in the form of annual dues from their respective members, as may be necessary for supporting the Grand Commandery.

No Subordinate Commandery shall confer the Orders of Knighthood for a less sum than twenty dollars.

There shall be a Contingent Fund of three hundred dollars, placed to the credit of the Most Eminent Grand Master, on the books of the Grand Treasurer, at the close of each triennial session ; out of which the Grand Master shall reimburse himself for his necessary cash expenses in the performance of his constitutional duties, and make a triennial report of the same to the Grand Encampment.

There shall be appropriated at each triennial session of the Grand Encampment of the United States, a sufficient sum to be used by the Grand Recorder to meet the current expenses of the Secretariat, of which he shall render an account at the succeeding session.

SECTION 2.—GENERAL REGULATIONS.

1. No Commandery, Grand or Subordinate, shall confer the Orders of Knighthood upon any one who is not a regular Royal Arch Mason, according to the requirements of the General Grand Chapter of the United States.

2. The rule of succession, in conferring the Orders of Knighthood, shall be as follows: 1. Knight of the Red Cross. 2. Knight Templar.

3. Every Commandery working in a State, District or Ter-

ritory, where there is a Grand Commandery, shall have a Dispensation or Charter from said Grand Commandery. And no Commandery hereafter to be formed or opened in such State, District, or Territory, shall be deemed legal without such Charter or Dispensation. All Masonic communication, as a Templar, is interdicted between any Commandery working under the general or special jurisdiction of this Grand Encampment, or any member thereof, and any Commandery or member of such, that may be formed, opened, or holden in such State, District, or Territory, without such Charter or Dispensation.

It shall be deemed irregular for any Commandery to confer the Orders of Knighthood, or either of them, upon any sojourner, whose settled place of residence is within any State, District, or Territory, in which there is a Commandery regularly at work, until the consent of the Commandery having territorial jurisdiction is first obtained. In the event of the violation of this interdict, the Commandery so offending, shall be subject to Knightly discipline, and be required, upon demand, to pay over to the Commandery thus defrauded, the amount of fees received for such admission.

The officers of every Commandery, Grand and Subordinate, before entering upon the exercise of their respective offices, shall take the following obligation, viz: "I, (A. B.) do promise and vow that I will support and maintain the Constitution of the Grand Encampment of Knights Templar of the United States of America."

The Grand Master of this Grand Encampment may issue his proxy to any Knight Templar in regular standing, authorizing him to constitute a Subordinate Commandery which has received a Charter; and any Commandery thus constituted, shall be deemed regularly constituted.

SECTION 3.—AMENDMENTS.

The Grand Encampment shall be competent upon the concurrence of three-fourths of its members present, at any stated meeting, to revise, amend, and alter this Constitution ; *provided*, one day's previous notice of such motion to amend be given, and a particular time be set to take the vote thereon.

In all other cases, any proposed amendment shall lay over until the next stated meeting of the Grand Encampment, when a concurring vote of two-thirds shall be necessary to adopt such alteration, amendment or revision.

SECTION 4.—RULES OF ORDER.

RULE 1.—After the ceremony of opening the Grand Encampment, it shall be the duty of the Grand Recorder to read the minutes of the last Triennial Session, unless such reading be dispensed with ; and at the resumption of business in each successive sitting, the minutes of the preceding one shall also be read.

RULE 2.—A Committee on Credentials, consisting of three Sir Knights, shall be appointed by the Grand Master, to report at the opening of the next sitting.

RULE 3.—After the report of this committee, the Grand Master, the Deputy Grand Master, the Grand Generalissimo, and the Grand Captain General, will successively read the reports of their doings during the preceding three years. These reports shall be referred to the Standing Committee on the doings of the Grand officers, who may recommend the apportionment of such parts thereof, to Special, or to such other of the Standing Committees, as they may deem necessary.

RULE 4.—The Standing Committees shall be :

1. A Committee on the Doings of the Grand Officers.
2. A Committee on Finance.
3. A Committee on Dispensations and New Commanderies.
4. A Committee on Unfinished Business.
5. A Committee on Grievances.
6. A Committee on Masonic Jurisprudence.
7. A Committee to designate the place of the next Triennial Meeting.

The report of these committees shall be heard in order, except the last one, which shall report on the last day of the meetings of the Grand Encampment.

RULE 5.—While the several committees are preparing their reports the new business may be acted upon ; and if any subject is brought forward requiring a reference to any Standing or Special Committee, it shall be so referred forthwith.   All committees shall make it a point to report as soon as convenient after their appointment.

RULE 6.—No Sir Knight shall be allowed to speak more than once on the same subject, except to explain the meaning of some of his remarks, unless it be by special permission of the Grand Encampment first obtained.

RULE 7.—The Grand Encampment shall proceed to the election of officers for the ensuing three years, immediately after the opening of the first sitting, on Thursday following the commencement of the Triennial Meetings.

RULE 8.—It shall be the duty of the Grand Master, at each Triennial Meeting, if time permit, to cause an exemplification of the work appertaining to the Orders of Knighthood to be exhibited before the Grand Encampment ; and also to correct, officially, all irregularities and discrepancies that exist.

> In testimony whereof I have caused the seal of the Grand Encampment to be hereunto affixed.
>
> Dated at the City of New Orleans, this 1st day of November, 1859, and of the Order, 741.

[L. S.]

> SAM'L G. RISK,
> *Grand Recorder.*

www.ingramcontent.com/pod-product-compliance
Lightning Source LLC
Chambersburg PA
CBHW021513090426
42739CB00007B/593